THE FOAL'S SEASONS

Linda Hartley

Photographs by Takeshi Kawamoto
GEC Garrett Educational Corporation

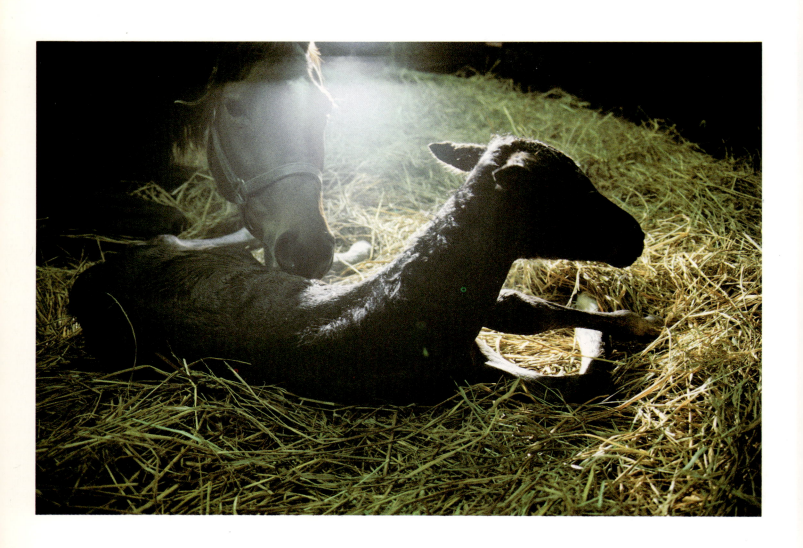

A foal is born.

The foal is cold

and hungry.

Its mother

gives warmth

and milk.

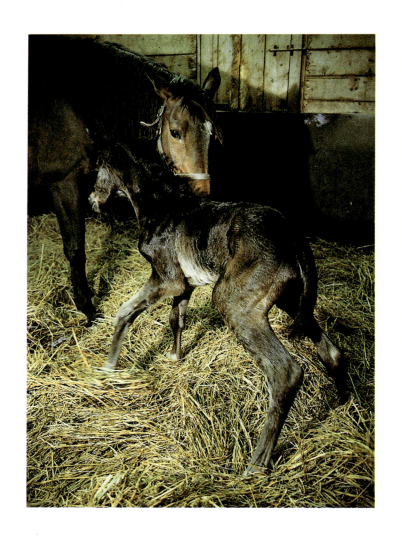

The foal goes outside

for the first time.

Look!

Other horses are

in the field.

The growing foal loves to race in the field.

It runs with other horses.

Snowy fields have become a sea of grass.

Spring is here.

The foal's body is growing.

It runs to keep up

with its mother.

A long day is over.

The mother horse and

young horse trot

toward the paddock.

The next morning

the young horse's life

is changed.

Its mother is led away.

The young horse

calls for its mother.

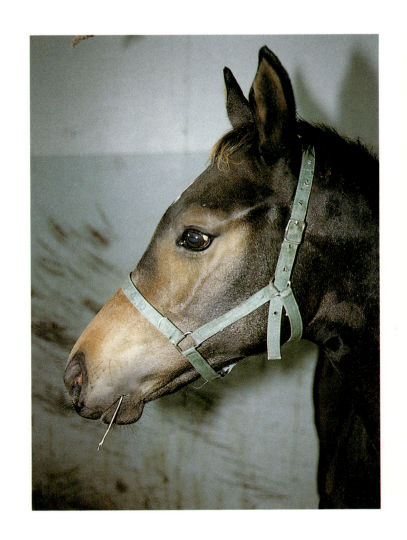

The mother horses are taken from their young.

This makes the foals grow strong.

The mother horses miss their young.

During warm
summer days,
the young horses
explore their world
together.

Soon the young horses run

and become strong and beautiful.

Edited by Eril Hughes
Text (c) 1996 by Garrett Educational Corporation

First Published in the United States in 1996 by Garrett Educational Corporation,
130 East 13th Street, Ada, Oklahoma 74820
Copyright 1987 Kaisei-Sha Publishing Co.

Manufactured in the United States of America

Hartley, Linda.
The Foal's seasons / Linda Hartley: photographs by Takeshi Kawamoto.
p. cm. - - (Shining nature)
Photographs originally published in: Kouma no shiki/Kawamoto Takeshi shashin. Tokyo: Kaiseisha, 1987, in series: Shizen kira kira.
Summary: Photographs and brief text follow a foal from birth through its growth to become a strong and beautiful horse.
ISBN 1-56074-069-8
1. Foals - - Juvenile literature. 2. Horses–Development–Juvenile literature. (1.Horses. 2. Animals–Infancy.) I. Kawamoto, Takeshi, 1944- ill. II. Kawamoto, Takeshi, 1944- Kouma no shiki. Selections. III. Title. IV. Series:
Hartley, Linda. Shining nature.
SF302.H4 1996
636.1'07- - dc20
96-27086
CIP
AC